Graceful Intentions

Mendi Hutchison

Presentation by *BookLeaf Publishing*

Web: www.bookleafpub.com

E-mail: info@bookleafpub.com

ISBN: 9789360941307

First edition 2024

I want to dedicate this book to my mother whom passed away in 2020. Your spirit and love has never left my side. I hold on to the memories of what special bond we had and I forever am grateful to be able to call you my Mother.

ACKNOWLEDGEMENT

I want to give a special heartfelt thanks to my two beautiful children whom inspire me daily to become the best version I can be. To live authentically and to love unconditionally.

PREFACE

The desire to live authentically becomes a way of life. The masks that were worn in situations where insecurity lived finally is not needed. Becoming one with the true essence of love is the light to your own purpose. Allowing presence to be the driving force of life and creativity. Flowing through your own inner guidance and wisdom. The limited beliefs that once held you back no longer controls your actions. The beauty of it all is the essence of peace that drives the alignment of your heart and mind. The purpose of life is about creation.

Solitude

This tiny cabin has led me to face just who I am
Being alone is what helped me grow
Because I had no one but me
The flowers that bloomed
The moon that peaked through the trees
The animals that roamed free
It was all me that sang a tune when I was blue
It was all me that wanted peace because I
believed I could find me
The dark sky
The stars that sparkled bright is what gave my
heart light
The beauty captivated me and the little sparkle
became bigger you see
My heart transformed as I sat with me
The love around me was always there
I created an illusion because I was in despair
The support I had was magical and true
I needed to first accept the mindset I outgrew
You do need to go within to grow
But you don't have to do it alone
The connection and presence of god Is the
universal flow

Rose-Colored Glasses

Love has been tainted by my rose colored toxic
trait
I felt it so purely but my heart always ended in a
break
I forgot about all the other stuff that ones
behavior has shown
In the end, I sat alone
Saying goodbye to the pain that kept me bound
is what I found truth in
This new vision was a new behavior I began
All I have ever wanted was to be seen as unique
as art
Maybe god will gift me with another's pure
heart.

The Last Kiss

3

Your lips are hot but your heart is cold
My arms grab your waist and hold you close
As I look deep into your eyes
I see your secret
I see your pain
I see your heart not wanting Cupid.

Intuitive Reflection

Your heart and mine
The strength of the energy intertwined
Your eyes shined bright but they were mine
The insight was brought through universal signs
The silence of the unspoken that was never
experienced before
The beauty it held kept me wanting more
Connected to oneself and mirrored as a
reflection
The simple truth of my own intuition

The Roots of the Inner Flame

5

The pain that seeps through my veins
Passion that still remains
Finding myself through an emotional connection
But losing myself through my own complexion.
How do I keep walking forward
When every turn I make I still feel cornered
I just want to surrender to all that I know
Each door I opened, is closed
Let my soul be free
Let me feel connected to those special to me
Allow my heart to breathe like the trees
So I can feel the fire within me

Free Spirited Beauty

Her green eyes shined so bright
Her freckles sparkled in the moonlight
Her colored hair was a beautiful sight
But what was captivating to me was the way her
spirit danced in the night
Seeing her face when the leaves fall
Seeing her face when the sun shines
Seeing her face when the snow gathers
Seeing her face with the sunflowers bloom
It was the magic she knew
It was the beauty her heart grew
Mostly it was the life she left behind
With her essence intertwined.

Emotionally Bound

My emotions are deep
Sometimes they cloud my mind
When I allow my ego to control them
I get further behind
Healing is a lifelong journey
There is always one more layer to see
But with each layer you uncover
Your heart feels more free

The Ocean's Tide

My emotions go as deep as the ocean
My words often go unspoken
I can't never find the words I need to say
To express the feelings I need to betray
When I do run across someone who cares
enough
I push them away because I try to be tough
I was taught wrong and now it's even harder to
change
The behaviors that were patterned are to blame
My ego fights but my heart wants to win
I'm not even sure where to begin
Allow me to find the words to speak
So I can feel my own inner peace

My Mothers Daughter

I am like my mother in many ways but I am
different too.
My strength lies in the healing I chose to pursue.
See I am a different version that gives to truth
I had to look at the illusions she grew
The ones she grew, I grew.
I kept all the pieces that she gave love too
This is what made her essence true.
I left the pain that broke her soul into
Be gentle to those who love so strong
The heart can believe in it so much that you do
yourself wrong.
I will always send my mother love because she
did the best she could
She loved me with the purest intentions no
matter what I understood.
I know this now but I had to heal and grow
She taught me something bigger that is true to
my soul.
I will always carry a piece of her with me in
everything I create
She was my mother and I am like her in many
ways.

Inner peace

The trees are dancing
The wind is howling
The rain storm is rolling in
The dark clouds surround me
As the birds fly away
While I stand here in the wind
Her eyes change like the ocean tide
The calmness they hold fills my heart with pride
Feeling the sand beneath my feet
Is a feeling my soul seeks
Its a feeling where my heart is free
Its a wisper of inner peace that consumes me

Empathic Heart

The emotions of others filled my heart
It was hard to separate them apart
I felt so deeply and didn't know how to express
Imagine living your whole life with this
heaviness in your chest
I had to separate myself so I could feel my own
But it also meant I had to walk alone
I learned establishing boundaries were essential
to me
So I could live a life with less toxicity.
Understanding myself through many painful
lessons
Has allowed me to appreciate my empathic heart
as a beautiful blessing

The fishing pole

This fishing pole is all I know
It keeps me up from dusk till dawn
My mind is clear with a hand full of beer
Knowing I have no where else to go

The simple life is what keeps my heart right
It's the only truth I know
I can see the clear water in front of me
All the fish swimming underneath my pole

This fishing pole is all I know
It keeps me up from dusk till dawn
My mind is clear with a hand full of beer
Just waiting for more fish to flow

The Calmness within the Storm

Live gives you moments
Where silence is peace
The fire you look into
Allows you to release

It's silence holds power
Your own calmness allows you to be
Its beauty holds truth
The moment allows your heart to be free

Presence overwhelms you
The serenity of a sound
It's just the crackling of wood
That makes your heart pound.

Wisdom of the Mind's Stillness

The sun shines upon you
As you absorb the view
Peace moves through your soul
You become more intentional and allow your life
to naturally flow
The freedom you feel becomes more important
than being trapped in the game
Your life's purpose becomes bigger than the
comfort of doing everything the same

Positive Alignment

15

There is so much beauty in this world that many
don't believe
It's what freed me from my darkest hour
I believed in the love that bridged my mind and
heart
I believed that there was good in everyone from
the start
I believed that no matter what I faced, I would
be fine
I believed the universe would work with me and
show me the signs
I found truth in many things
I cut many negative strings
Fear is just an illusion that our mind creates
It can put you in a stagnate mental state.
Believe what you want to believe and I will
believe you too
The mind will create a reality that suits you

Universal Surrender

16

Universe take me where I need to go
Allow my heart to openly flow
Allow me to live in the present moment
Allow me to change my perspective so I am
mentally free
But Mostly allow me to open my eyes to see the
beauty that surround me
Not just the big things but the small things too
The birds that cross my path
The trees that softly blow in the wind
Allow me to breath with passion
But with it all……
Allow me live with purpose

Divinity

17

The stars that sparkle
The sun that shines
The moon that glimmers
The deep conversations
The smell of a sweet flower
The eyes that are deeply Divine
The ocean that goes on forever
The sand that fills between your toes
The presence of being
To love, to create, and to be authentic
To connect, to be present and to feel
Living with each breathe
Being one with divinity.

This Old Cabin

It's hard to let go
My heart fills with sorrow
The beauty that takes my breath away
Makes my heart want to stay
I know it's time to go
Because my intuition tells me so
I can choose to stay
But my personal growth might delay
Life is about constant change
Focusing your attention is true
Seeing a new vision
Creating a new you
I fell in love once again
With something that was never mine to begin
This cabin needed so much work
It was a reflection of my own heart when it was
broke
I gave it love and made it my own
But now I have to say goodbye and let it go
The ground that was covered with trees was a
reflection of me
The animals that roamed made my heart feel
free
I will continue to grow
By allowing my life to naturally flow

There is beauty in that I see
This is what I learned in this old cabin buried
within the trees.

Cutting the Strings

The hardest lesson in life is letting go
It's powerful and true and needed for growth
Being in love is beautiful but it's never enough
It can pull on your heart strings and become
painfully tough
If you don't have the the same vision to make a
relationship work
It will become toxic and you will leave with
your heart broke.

Deep Soul Love

Love will find its way to you if it's true
Otherwise it will become absent to you
It is like a calmness and a fire that takes over the
soul
The heart beats stronger as time goes
Its different than the toxic ways you might know
It's deeper and it aligns with your soul
A higher soulmate some would say
A twin flame, a term many use today
I couldn't say
I do know one truth
It will be a love you both have to choose
It points you back to yourself so you can grow
You might not understand it at first but
eventually you will know
Love will find its way to you if it's true

The Graceful Flower

22

Leaving parts of my old self and creating new
Finding peace with the small things I do
Living a life that is heart-centered too
Finding joy in the presence of life
Finding creative ways to write
Living by allowing my creative flow
But mostly finding my purpose in the unknown.
You water the seeds as you watch them grow
When you let go, you surrender to your soul.
Captivated by its own unique artistic flow
Femininity is like a flower that moves with
grace
While its beauty holds power that you softly
embrace.